Words
Of
Comfort

A Collection Of Poems And Inspirational Writings

By

E. D. Arrington

First published by AuthorHouse 3/20/2006.

ISBN: 1-4259-0962-0 (sc)
Printed in the United States of America
Bloomington, Indiana.

Book Design: EWS and Associates
Cover Design: Tamika Day

Books By E. D. Arrington

Stay The Course

On The Edge

*Words Of Comfort: A Collection Of Poems
And Inspirational Writings*

Coming Soon!

*On The Edge – R e v i s i t e D
(The Continuing Saga Of On The Edge)*

*Forever Was A Day
(The Sequel To Stay The Course)*

Reading...A Pathway To The Heart

Dedicated To

Tom ("Deddi")   And   Eva ("Ma") Brown

Arrington

A Note From The Author

Words Of Comfort: A Collection Of Poems And Inspirational Writings comes primarily as a result of requests from family and friends seeking a special way to honor the memory of their loved ones. Though this is my first collection of poems and inspirational writings, it has proven to be my most rewarding genre, for it has allowed me to enter into the innermost part of my being — revealing, tapping into, bringing to the surface tender emotions that have been safely tucked away from others, and, in some cases, from myself. Writing *Words Of Comfort* has lifted me to new horizons as a person, as a woman, as a spiritual being. It has been cathartic and has affirmed the old sayings that the energy we put out returns to us; and, that so often, when you think what you're doing is a blessing to others, can actually turn out to be a blessing to you.

But what I cherish most in writing this book of poetry is having been given the incredible opportunity to honor life — the lives of so many wonderful people who I knew personally and loved unconditionally.

So as you read each poem, each letter of inspiration — my greatest wish is that you find calm, peace, and joy in my *Words Of Comfort*.

Best Wishes,

E. D. Arrington

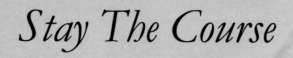

Stay The Course

A Tribute To Our Beloved Women

True Beauty Dwells Within

When You Think Of Me

Remembering My Mother, My Mentor , My Best Friend

When the curtains are drawn bringing this day to an end
One darest to wonder the distance in time
When or if we will see each other again
But the moments we have shared will not soon fade, you see
They shall linger on in the deep recesses of our minds
A milestone in history
So when you replay these memories for all the world to see
This is what I ask you to remember when you think of me

A picturesque sun rising to welcome in a new day
A full moon setting allowing darkness its moment to play
A cool soothing breeze caressing summer parched skin
A gentle hand cupping a baby's tiny soft chin
A mighty wave rolling across a shimmering blue sea
A child's squealing burst of laughter bouncing upon my knee
A picnic with someone special in the park shaded by
    a tall oak tree
Yes, this is what I ask you to remember
    when you think of me

A rainbow fanning its colors across a brilliant cloudless sky
A flock of eagles spreading their wings soaring oh so high
The sweet smell of freshly wet dirt cleansed by
    an April shower
A lone walk by the edge of the river
Not for a hurried moment, but for a leisurely hour
Bright yellow roses dancing upon a bed of lush green grass
Honey bees swarming free for the first time
    from their caged nest
A spring bouquet perfuming the air
A butterfly adorning your hair
The sheer pleasure of recalling the joys that used to be
Now, this is what I ask you to remember
    when you think of me

A beautifully written story with a beautifully written end
Of a life of hope, best wishes with no more broken
    hearts to mend
An old favorite song, a new dance, love that abounds
That was always within an arm's reach just
    waiting to be found
Along the journey we traveled with the quest
    to fulfill life's destiny
For being our best is all we could ever hope to be
So when your mind wonders back over our days
    spent so fondly
Yes, this is what I ask you to remember
    When You Think Of Me.

A Moment Just For You

In Celebration Of Your Special Day

In the midst of your elegance, beauty and charm
We stand before you four generations strong
To honor you in word and in praise
To celebrate a life that leaves one thoroughly amazed
So just sit back for a second — maybe two
For this is a moment just for you

Through the years you have been there
With encouraging words, warm embraces
A gentle hand to wipe the tears from our faces
Your sternness or steely strength that showed mightily outside
Could not hide the depth of your compassion that abides inside

Your love was not limited to shape, size or the color of skin
With outstretched hands, you helped whomever, however or when
For when God made you He made a jewel
Then showed you favor to be used as His tool
To share the blessings He so plentifully bestowed
That you may help others come in from the cold

Without you — no we darest not to wonder what our lives would be
For you've brought us more than our wildest imagination could see
More excitement than a ride on a raging sea
Or an ocean's wild wave bounding endlessly
More joy than stars in a magnificent cloudless sky
Why we've been so blessed? Only God knows why
And the love, the fun, the joy is hardly over — no we're not through
On this special day all fresh and brand new
We've set aside this time — A Moment Just For You.

My Friend

When my legs were too weak
You helped me stand
When mine no longer worked
You lent me your hand
When my eyes refused to see
You cleared the way
Bravely guiding me through the darkness
Into the light of another new day

Listening with compassionate ears
You banished the pain of many years

Nurtured gaping wounds
Dried a flood of endless tears
So,
Who stayed closer than skin?
Who remained steadfast through the thick and the thin?
Who helped me through each new challenge again and again?
Who rejoiced in my every win?
Who weathered my storm to the very end?
Who loved me dearer than any blood kin?
With a heart full of thanks, behind a joy-filled grin
I answer simply:
My Friend.

To You, My Dear, Mother

A Mother's Day Wish

Good Morning, Mother
I come in honor of you on this special day
With a heart overflowing in exaltation and praise
Bearing gifts and words of thanks for all you've done for me
To commemorate your very being, for leading me when I could not see
    down a road replete with challenges, obstacles, bumps and curves
It was you who knew when to duck, to sway, and to swerve
    from the dangers that lay in wait, you had the wisdom to discern
And from your patience and gracious teachings, I, too, came to understand and learn

Good Afternoon, Mother
The day is already halfway through
And I have yet to share all I desire with you
There remain many precious memories I eagerly wish to recall
The fun times we spent together when I was oh so very small
Like the day my tears flowed one early morn while you tenderly nursed my knee
That I had scraped, cut and bruised from being where I wasn't supposed to be

Good Evening, Mother
I must soon bid farewell for this day has grown nigh
When sharing unforgettable moments with you, my, my how the times does fly
Come let me tuck you in bed for your much needed sleep
And as you lay down your head, I'll pray the Lord your soul to keep
Watching you rest so peacefully is such a beautiful sight
Sweet dreams, my dear, mother
Happy Mother's Day
Good night.

The Power Of Silence

My smile beamed wide on our wedding day
But by night's end, you had smacked it away
With a fist that came crashing painfully against my face
My first lesson, you said, was to learn my rightful place

Yet, when morning came, you whispered tenderly
With convincing words that the real problem was me
All was forgiven for what seemed truly a mystery
Our life could now go on, you said, the way it was meant to be

Ten years later, I still sit cowering helplessly
Nothing has changed…well, except for me
    I'll not move a muscle
    No I'll not blink an eye
    I'll not so much as dare to cry
    As you go stomping by

You've taught me my last lesson
Tonight, I'll count my blessing
Though, for you, I think I still feel love, or maybe it's sympathy
But this plan, my dear, will include only me
So you just go ahead ranting, raving, spewing out your violence
    For when daylight dawns
    I'll be long gone
    You see, I've learned The Power Of Silence.

An Ending Of A Similar Kind

A Poem Just For You

I looked into your eyes and saw mine
The countenance of your face sent me traveling back in time
The love that poured from your heart reminded me of another
It was the same love I had shared with my mother
On a hot muggy August morn my mother went away
My age, too, was young and tender
But I can clearly remember
     that day

I woke to a world that
     suddenly felt enormously
     big and round
And I, like the tiniest ant,
     now seemed too small
     to ever be found
I wondered how or if I would
     again have a place
     where I belong
For my mother was gone, my
     life no longer had its song

Then one magnificent morn, I
     woke to a brand new world
One filled with hopes and dreams meant just for this little girl
So I dug in my heels and went searching
     for all I could discover
Eager to see what possibilities lay ahead
Each I wanted to uncover

The road I traveled surely was not easy
There were many dips, twists, bumps and curves
Many times I nearly quit
Many times I nearly lost my nerves
     during those dark, scary moments when it
     didn't feel much like I was winning

But with an iron will and a soul
     full of hope,
I leaped in and sent myself
     spinning on a journey with no
     light, no map, no direction sign
Just sheer determination to find
     the life destined to be mine

Though, I'm much older, there
     remains much more I
     want to do
And on the very top of my list
     was to write this poem
     just for you
To leave a message that I pray
     you'll always keep close in
     mind
For along your life's journey, you may face a string of
     endless struggles
But if you refuse to quit, refuse to give up
     each and every time
One bright early morn, you, too,
     will rise beneath a sea of stars to find
That we not only share a story with a familiar beginning
     But with An Ending Of A Similar Kind.

One Day

A Time For Reflection

One day, I'll see Jesus
One day, I'll have my meeting with God
One day, I'll take my place in Glory
On that Great Day, I'll be going home

Oh, now, you don't have to worry
For I've already made my peace with the Lord
You see, where I'm going there'll be
no more pain or struggle
On that Great Day, only rest will
fill my soul

I'm going to that place He prepared for me
Oh, no, no I won't be alone
Those who have gone on before me
Will be there waiting, waiting to welcome me home

One day, I'll see Jesus
One day, I'll have my meeting with God
One day, I'll take my place in Glory
On that Great Day, I'll be going home.

Her Moment To Rest

There will be another sunrise
There will be another sunset
There will be another rainbow
As a reminder of the promise
He intended us never to forget

There will be another flood
Washing our lovely gardens away
There will be another blanket of snow of light fluffy flakes
Giving the children another occasion to play

There will be another illness baffling us all
There will be another hurt, another pain
That will touch the big and the small
There will be another laughter, another tear, another joy, another fear
There will be another struggle, another challenge, another test
There will be another time when God's hand will reach out and touch
Summoning another mother for Her Moment To Rest.

Before You Pull That Shade

Just one second God
Before you pull that shade
Been laying here doing some thinking
Got a few more things to say

Children, remember those lessons that I taught
Pass them along to my grandbabies
    so they'll know the battle that I fought

Just one second God
Before you pull that shade
Much is still roaming around in this old head
Some that has never been said

Children, I sure do appreciate the kindness
    I was shown
I thank you from the bottom of my heart
And many mornings it was what gave me
    that little extra start
Knowing you were in my corner to the very last mile
Could light my face up nearly all day with one
    of my pretty old smiles

Just one second God
Before you pull that shade
I know I'm going on a bit long
But I've got one more thing to say

Children, I won't be there to listen to your stories
    or your complaints

Or those jokes you thought were so funny
Or your woes about this and that, friends,
    cars and money
But not for one moment will you be far from the
    warmth of my tender heart
For it is where I planted my love for you right
    from the very start

Just one second God
Before you pull that shade
Let me say this for I would be remiss
And without further ado
I promise you I will be through

Children, you all look out for
    one another like loving kin
As you travel along your journey,
    make God your best friend
Well…God is calling me
I must say my goodbye for now
I love you, I'll miss you and I want you to always
    remember this
God soothes wounds, wipes tears and broken hearts
    He will mend
I'm a witness, in any storm, it is He
    who will see you to the end
So you take comfort in all that
    I have said and in knowing
Like falls' colorful leaves whisked
    together by a rush of gentle wind
We, my dear loved ones, will see each other again

Okay, God
My bed's all made
Go ahead
Pull my shade.

I'm All Right

Walk slowly out onto the porch
Step ever so close to the very edge
Now look over your shoulder just to the right
Did you see that spark brighter
    than the moon's glowing light?

Walk slowly down the steps
Stop at the landing where the grass presses gently
    against your toes
Now bend low ever so carefully
Pick up that lone white tissue
Did you smell the pretty scent of a rose tickle your nose?

Walk slowly into the house
Pause only to turn off the light
Climb quietly into bed
Tuck yourself in real tight
Did you think sleep would abandon you on this
    particular night?

No, let not sleep abandon you on this night or any other
You see, each one of those signs came from me
Yes, your loving mother
I was there with you on the porch
Remember that spark brighter than the moon's glowing light?
I was there with you on the landing where the grass presses
    gently against your toes
Remember the pretty scent of a rose tickling at your nose?

It was my turn to have my last say
To take my last bow before I went on my way
A last tender moment to ease your mind while we're apart
A last reminder that you'll always be planted forever
    in my heart

So the next time the pretty scent of a rose
    tickles your nose
Or you see a spark brighter
    than the moon's glowing light
Though I'm no longer within your reach
And for a short while out of your sight
Your mother is at rest in God's peaceful sleep
Yes, my dear, loved ones – I'm All Right.

When The Morning Comes

Don't hide from it
No, don't you run
From the sorrow, from the grief
Yes, let it come
Feel every hurt, every ache, every tinge of pain
Let your tears flow down your cheeks
Like a torrential pouring rain

Don't hide from it
No, don't you run
From the shock, from the anger
Yes, let it come
Feel each moment of disbelief, each moment of stun
Let your heart break for your loved one is gone

Don't hide from it
No, don't you run
From your new beginning
Yes, let it come
Let the night give way to a fresh new day
Where all of your weeping got washed away
Feel His peace from your long needed rest
Feel His relief for you have stood the test
Then wake early as God's glorious sun slowly dawns
For there you will find joy, unspeakable joy, yes,
beautiful joy
When The Morning Comes.

Joy In The Midst Of Sorrow

A man drowning in grief cried out in
frustration – God!
Where Are You? What Are You? Who Are
You?

And God Answered:

I am the bluest sky before the hurricane
I am the rainbow bursting with color
After the heavy rain
I am the healing ointment
For the wounded heart in despair

I am the warm gentle breeze
Shielded from the cold frenzied air
I am the calm riding life's ocean
Of bumpy rolling waves
I am the hope that binds destined never to fade
I am the happy bubble wherever trouble abounds
I am the lift in the spirit whenever pain is found

On the longest walk shadowed by the loneliest moments
I am the glow of light that brightens
the darkest hour
I am the bloom of the loveliest flower
I am the gate that shuns the dread of
having to face tomorrow
I am the Joy In The Midst Of Sorrow.

A Tribute To The Life Of Ruby Swinson-Sanford

I was not more than five years old when we met. It was on a Saturday. I went visiting in Stantonsburg, North Carolina, with Ma and Deddi, my grandmother and grandfather. While they did their weekly grocery shopping, they sent me to sit on the front porch of the home of my stepfather, Aaron Swinson. I sat down in a green swing chair next to this high-yellow, big forehead little girl. She was wearing black eyeglasses, sucking her thumb, and digging in her navel. "What's your name?" I asked the little girl, eager to make a new friend. She gave me an annoyed, under-eyed stare over a pair of thick-lens glasses. "Ruby," she said, after an intentional pause, and turned her head in the other direction.

About two years later, we found ourselves attending the same school – North Greene Elementary…the first grade class of 1959. During recess, I spotted the high-yellow, big forehead, black eyeglasses-wearing little girl on the playground standing by herself, while the other children ran wild, playing, laughing, and talking. I naïvely scurried over to her and said, "Hey. You wanna play?" She paused and gave me the same annoyed under-eyed stare over her thick-lens eyeglasses. "No," she said, matter-of-factly, and looked down at the ground.

But somewhere between the first grade and the eighth grade, Ruby chose me to be one of her dearest friends. In 1968, the year my grandmother died, I was sent to live with Aunt Bessie in Alexandria, Virginia. Twenty-five and some years later, I retired and returned to my home state of North Carolina. It was then that Ruby told me how angry she was when I moved away and vowed never to speak to me again. Of course, I reminded my dear friend that I had no choice in the matter, which she reluctantly conceded. After a few foolish arguments, debates, and butting of heads, Ruby gradually put aside what she called her *hurt feelings* and we resumed a friendship that the years, arguments, and *hurt feelings* could not fade.

Once we got past some little – no, BIG hurdles – Ruby Swinson-Sanford telephoned me whenever she got a notion to talk – seven o'clock in the morning, eight o'clock in the morning. But I put my foot down when she asked if it was all right to call me at three o'clock in the morning. I said, "Girl, you better not call me that early in the morning." She said, "Don't you ever wake up just wanting to talk to somebody?" And I said, "Not at three o'clock in the morning! At three o'clock in the morning, I don't know if I'm alive, and I don't want you to call to find out." She roared with laughter.

Ruby and I shared an honest friendship, a true friendship, a genuine friendship. We gave each other the green light to speak our minds, to say what was in our hearts, while the other was obligated to listen…but with the freedom to disagree without anger. Now, of course, that didn't always work. For Ruby was a little stubborn…well, a lot stubborn. For Ruby wanted to have her way at times…well, most of the time. For Ruby liked to have the last word occasionally…well, more than occasionally. The truth is, Ruby had to have the last word. And, so did I.

For four years, Ruby and I talked sometimes four, five, six, seven…if I answered the phone, ten times a week. Those conversations opened the door to a side of Ruby people seldom got to know. Conversations that allowed me to see past the rough, tough outer surface into her heart – a heart filled with love and the desire to be loved, to be understood, to matter.

Often during our conversations, I focused on my relationship with my grandmother. Ruby would listen intensely as I would go on and on about the sacrifices my grandmother made for her seven grandchildren, and the depth of my love and appreciation I held for Eva Brown-Arrington – a lady who gave up so much in hopes that I

might have a chance for a better life. Now that I was older, I understood clearly the challenges and the sacrifices my Ma made, her never-ending commitment and the love she gave selflessly to everyone of her grandchildren – grandchildren that she cherished, grandchild that gave her life purpose and meaning, grandchildren that fueled her desire to face the challenges of another day. I was now witnessing all that in my friend, Ruby, who was determined to do the same for her four grandchildren. Seldom did talk of my grandmother ever seem to bore Ruby. Actually, it seemed to inspire her to try even harder. And seldom did we end a phone call after such a talk that Ruby didn't fail to say, "Lois, when I hear you talk about Ms. Eva, all I pray is that my grandchildren will love me the way you love her." With confidence, I responded to my friend by saying, "Ruby, they already do. Your grandchildren love you every bit as much. Trust me, they do."

That opened the door for me to remind Ruby that no matter what anyone else accomplished in life, no matter how many material gains are realized, no job was harder and should garner more respect than the work she did every day raising her four grandchildren. And Ruby, without fail, before hanging up from our phone conversations, ended by saying, "I love you so much, girl." I would say, "I love you, too, Ruby." And I did.

Whenever I Learn Another Mother Is Gone

My Dear Friend, Mary Jo:

Whenever I learn another mother is gone, I can't help but think back to the day my mother passed away. I think about having to face the pain of losing her – about having to say goodbye at a time when I was just ready to say hello. I think about how we were beginning to enter into that place – a place, I believe, all mothers look forward to entering with their daughters…that place called friendship.

Whenever I learn another mother is gone, I think back to those times I would wake with something on my mind that I needed to tell my mother only to remember she was no longer here. Words could not describe how much I missed her. Talking to her picture was not the same. Sitting by her gravestone pouring out my heart was not the same. There was nothing and no one who could take her place. No ears could hear me like my mother. No mouth could form the right words at the right time in the right way like my mother. No hands could touch me or feel like my mother. There was no love as deep, as gentle, as soothing, as understanding like my mother's love.

Whenever I learn another mother is gone, I think back to the many times when I cried out in pain, anger, grief, frustration, loneliness, sadness. Then one day those tears changed. Now when I cry, I cry tears of joy, praise, wonderment, and thanksgiving. Thanks to God for having blessed me with such a wonderful mother. That our lives together had formed so many good memories and filled my heart with so many glorious moments with an abundance of love – enough love to last me ten lifetimes. Now I cry tears of appreciation for every touch, every smile, every word of wisdom my mother bestowed upon me through His grace and His teachings. In those moments of calm, of introspection, and spiritual meditation, I can feel my mother's presence as if she was right here with me. She guides me, supports me, encourages me, whispers to me and sometimes scolds me – her spirit to my spirit. Amazing, I thought I had lost her when she was with me all along.

Although, my friend, we now share an experience of a similar kind, I still cannot say that I *know* the depth of *your* pain. But the day will come when your grieving will subside giving way to the beauty that waits to emerge. And on that day, a rush of memories, wonderful memories, joyful memories, indescribable memories will flood you like a river at high tide.

The Simple Things

In Memory Of A Special Wife, A Special Daughter, A Special Friend

Dear Dietrich:

Whether experienced one or one hundred and one times, be it a close loved one or a passing acquaintance, be it sudden or knowingly anticipated – death rocks the very foundation that most of us so firmly stand on.

Pain – the gripping pain from such a loss – rips through our hearts, clawing at every fiber of our being, twists, pulls, and tugs at our every emotion. Yet, it is in the throws of such emotion that we often strive to remember our departed in grandiose fashion. We applaud their academic achievements and various degrees of scholarship – high school diploma, B.A. M.A., Ph.D., J.D., D.D.S. We highlight their noteworthy affiliations – sororities, fraternities, committee appointments, organizational connections, outstanding employment history, and charitable, philanthropic contributions. All these merit honorable mention, and are of some relative importance.

Oh, but when I think of Ethel Roberta Ham-Thompson ("Bert"), I am engulfed by, saturated with, immersed in the simple things. With her head slightly tilted back, her mouth opened just wide enough to allow the escape of her thunderous laughter, her eyes sparkling as bright as the midday sun, her gentle touch, her warm embrace – her greeting to all was the same…a genuine hello, an offer of something to drink – a nice big glass of ice cold water.

When I think of Bert, I picture a small child being lulled into a deep sleep by the soothing tap, tap, tapping of rain against an old tin roof, the wondrous smell of fresh sweet wet soil peppering the air seconds after a downpour, a long slow walk through a thick mass of wet hunter green grass behind the backdrop of a deep blue sky.

Bert was a wonderful human being, a loyal and devoted wife, a loving daughter, a prized granddaughter, a precious sister, a favorite aunt, a dear cousin, a best friend. When I think of Bert, I think of those important, those irreplaceable, and yes, those things often overlooked – *The Simple Things*.

Remembering Your Mother, My Friend

Dear Denise:

I met your mother in the parking lot of the Stonehedge community in Silver Spring, Maryland. It was the late 1980s. Ruth was getting out of her blue Mazda just as I came speeding up in my brown Chevrolet. I had seen her coming and going, but until that day we had not exchanged a single word. That day, Ruth waited by her car. Her skin was radiant, every hair in place and every stitch of clothing settled neatly on her youthful body. A smile crept across her face. Her sparkling bright eyes greeted me first. "Hey girl," Ruth said as I got out of my car. We made small talk, much of which I now cannot remember. Of course, we exchanged names, learned that we were both mothers and were both trying to settle in our new homes.

We continued our meetings as we passed in the parking lot, sharing brief, pleasant greetings, an occasional chat about new happenings in and around the neighborhood, or the hectic world we lived in until one summer night of 1992. That night, Ruth paid me my first visit at home –a short visit. As she was about to leave, she paused at the door, turned and said, "Ethel, write down my

telephone number, girl. If there's anything I can ever do for you, just let me know. I mean it, now." I thanked Ruth for the visit, wrote down her telephone number and gave her mine.

That was the beginning. I don't know who made the first call or what we talked about. What I do know is that we made history. We might even belong in the Guinness Book of World Records because Ruth and I talked every single day about something. We shared books, debated the selections by Oprah's book club, and rated and sparred over our own interpretation of books we read.
Often we agreed, other times we didn't. But never did I hang up from a conversation with Ruth not looking forward to our next talk. My conversations with her left me feeling more informed, uplifted, and joyful. She brought light – much light to my life.

When I began my own quest to write a novel, Ruth read every manuscript with as much interest and enthusiasm as if I was her own daughter. She encouraged me and was overjoyed that I had found something that I loved. She was the first person to tell me, "Ethel, one day you're going to get published." And only if my heart could speak could anyone ever know how greatly I was inspired by her belief in me…a belief that came right from the very start. And the good Lord only knows, now when I look back on some of my old manuscripts, what Ruth saw. (They were bad!) But I'm glad I had her in my corner, rooting me on, believing in me, giving me that extra bit of support we all sometimes need.

In 1999, Ruth called to tell me that you, Denise, were getting married. Soon after, she called to say that you and your new husband, Henry, had found a beautiful house in South Carolina and would be moving away. Selfishly, I secretly wished that you would not get married. Ruth and I had shared so much together, our happy moments, sad moments, our ups and downs with our health. I didn't want to face the thought of her not being right around the corner. But that day did come when you packed and I was forced to watch my dear friend, Ruth, move away from her home in Silver Spring, Maryland to make a new beginning in South Carolina. That day, when I had to say goodbye, I felt my heart crumble into a hundred pieces. I grieved tremendously. I cried to my sister and to my best friend, Fredi, over what I considered one of my biggest losses. And then one night, not more than a week later, while sitting in my den, the phone rang. It was Ruth. We picked up right where we left off. No, we didn't talk as long or as often as we once did. But after every conversation I was left feeling just as informed, just as hopeful, just as joyful as before. Ruth had moved to another state, but nothing about our friendship had changed.

Ruth and I often shared our views on race relations, education, childrearing, world politics and religion. Her faith in God was unshakeable. A part of her daily routine was to read the Bible in the morning and at night before bed. Many times she said to me, "Ethel, I'm not worried about dying. I know I'm going to be with Jesus." When I wrote the poem, *One Day*, I thought about Ruth. And now, when I read it, I'm more than certain it is a testament to her strong faith.

Ruth was not shy about letting me know how much she loved her children – you, Denise, and Patrick. In one of our last conversations, she told me how happy she was that you married Henry. She said, "Ethel, they are both so loving to me. I couldn't have asked for a better daughter. Denise is good to me. I don't have to worry about a thing." The remainder of our conversation centered on Rusty, the dog you gave Ruth as a gift. I can't say I have ever met anyone who loved a pet as much as Ruth loved Rusty. She even wrote a poem about him entitled, *Bad As I Wanna Be*. During our phone conversations, she spent as much time talking to Rusty as to me. He brought her such joy. And the joy in her life is how Ruth wanted to be remembered. So when you think of her, think of a blue sky, a brilliant sun, a calm ocean, a radiant big smile – for the Ruth I know and loved is smiling.

A Tribute To Our Beloved Men

The Things I Never Got To Say

Happy Father's Day

I saw you lying there so peaceful and still
Ma said it was your time
That it was God's will
It was then I realized on that very day
All the things I never got to say

Sweat poured from your brow
From working the fields, holding the plow
Tilling the soil from dusk to dawn
To put food on the table since the day
    I was born

Tinker and tinker you did on that old car
For the little money you made didn't
    go very far
You stretched yourself thin sacrificing
    to make do
Because the weather was turning cold
And I needed a new pair of shoes

I saw the tears you tried to hide
The pain you felt you kept buried inside
Even when you were mad you never
    shouted out loud
And though you were a man of few words
Of me, I knew you were proud

On Sunday mornings, didn't you look
    handsome in that dark blue suit
And the way you laughed was some
    kind of cute

A simple man were you, not perfect at all
Who loved watching TV and playing baseball

If you were here right now, I'd hug you real tight
And play checkers with you well past midnight
But before I would go off to bed
I'd stop along the way
And tell you all The Things I Never Got To Say.

A Season For Pause

In every life there comes a
    season for pause —
A pause cradled in laughter
    and tears
That spanned a life through
    many years
A pause filled with
    happiness and sorrow
Tucked in the deep recesses
    of our hearts
For a quick peek in
    yesterday, today, and
    tomorrow

In every life there comes a
    season for pause —
A pause where precious
    memories get filed away
Where they can be stroked
    and caressed day after day
        the sound of your voice when you talk
        the uniqueness of your step, the way you walk
        the smile in your eyes, the shape of your lips
        the rhythm of your glide, the swagger in your hips

In every life there comes
    a season for pause —
A pause to savor your
    tender touch
To sing your praises for
    you've done so very
    much that made a
    difference in many
    lives without
    questions, wonders,
    whens, wheres or
    whys

In every life there comes a
    season for pause —
A pause to have our
    final goodbye
To allow in the pain, to
    have that last cry
But ask not for a reason nor search out the cause
For in every life there comes A Season For Pause.

A Moment Of Splendor

The years took back the
    agility of my mind
My body grew frail with
    passing time
But nothing could rob the
    smile from my face
You see, I could still feel
    your warm embrace
And just when I was
    about to draw my last
    breath
That place where some
    folks think there's
    nothing left
I was flooded with my
    life's memories
Aaah, yes, the beauty of
    the way things used
    to be.

Remember When:
We took long walks under the moonlit sky
We sat on the porch holding hands in the summer sun
    watching our friends ride by
We worked the fields until the day was gone
And stayed up half the night rubbing our tired, sore bones
Then rose early the next morning looking forward to a
    brand new day
Because we had each other to help pave the way

Remember When:
We started our family of daughters and sons
You placed each one in my arms the day they were born

I held them close if but
    for a little while
I can still feel the warmth
    of every child
The pleasures of my life
    that came rushing
    back in my last breath
That place where some
    folks think there's
    nothing left
Well, my memories are far
    too many to reveal
So take those that I've
    shared as a measure
    of the joy I feel

And in your time of quiet when you think of me
These are the thoughts I wish yours to be
That of hearty laughter absent of tears
Melodic music soothing to the ears
Our never-ending love so warm and tender
A life well spent is what I ask you to remember

For when I released my final breath
That place where some folks think there's nothing left
I did not for a second pause or hinder
Nor to fear did I surrender
Though my departure here does mark an ending
Something new and magnificent is just beginning
That mere words alone cannot express or render
For this is nothing less than A [sheer] Moment Of Splendor.

The Beauty In My Silence

My voice has been quieted
Never again shall an utterance be heard
Lift your hand, place it over your heart
It is there we will share our special moments
    now that we are apart

My footsteps have been made still
Not by mine, but by His will
Oh, but if you could see the smile on my face
You would get your bags ready for your journey
    to this place

My weeping is forever hushed
Narry a tear will I again wipe away
And should your eyes refuse to run dry
Remember these words I leave with you today

My sorrow is forever gone
My struggle is in the past
My suffering is over and done
For I have endured my very last
So in your pause when you remember me
Don't wish for the way things used to be
I'm at home safe from hurt, harm or violence
Sssssssssh... listen....
It is there where you will find
The Beauty In My Silence.

I Don't Know

I don't know your pain
I only know mine
I don't know your sorrow
But I've been visited by a similar kind

I don't know the obstacles that have fallen your way
Though I have had my share of struggles
    each and every day
I don't know the taste of your salty tears
Yet, I have cried many over the years

I don't know how long your hurt will last
Mine still comes and goes as if refusing to let go of the past
I don't know the day when you will laugh out loud again
I do remember though that bright sunny morn
    when my laughter began

I don't know when you'll stop calling out his name
    expecting to hear a returning refrain
I don't know the many times you will be certain
    you saw the smile on his face
    unable to recall the exact time or place

I don't know how you should say goodbye to the man
    you've loved since a baby boy
The memories are far too many of home, life, fun and joy
Nothing or no one can fill the space in your heart
    that for him will remain void
You must seek strength to face this challenge from our God
    and our Lord

So I pass along this verse from Psalms Thirty and Five
Just a few words that continue to keep my spirit alive
"Tears may flow in the night but joy cometh in the morning"
Just you continue to hold tight for your day
    is quickly dawning.

When You've Done Your Best

When you've done your best
Your tears will last for only a little while
When you've done your best
Loved ones already know you went that extra mile
When you've done your best
Your heartache soon makes way for a happy smile
When you've done your best
This part of life will now reside in the
'fondly remembrance' file

When you've done your best
You did all that you can
When you've done your best
It is a grand feat of accomplishment for any man
When you've done your best
Nothing more from you can anyone ask or demand
When you've done your best
With both feet planted, hold yourself steady,
with clear eyes, a clear mind, and clean hands
Rise and proudly stand.

Goodbye Old Friend

A Letter To A Wonderful Neighbor

Dear Joe:

It is truly hard to say goodbye, old friend. You were unique…one of a kind. You were the kind of neighbor that doesn't come along every day. There were no guessing games when it came to you, Joe. You were always the same…gentle and kind, strong and forceful, compassionate and loving, concerned and caring. You loved people – good people – regardless of race, sex, or age. None of that mattered.

And although you endured disabling back pain for years, did that stop you from making the most of every day? Of course, not. And when you discovered the seriousness of your illness, did you throw up your hands and give up? No – you fought back. You showed us strength, bravery and courage. But there's more. Yes, Joe, you left us with so much more.

You taught us what it meant to be a good human being. You shoveled your neighbor's walkway when she was too sick…never mind if your back would hurt the rest of the week. You watched out for our homes whether we were on our jobs, out of town, inside asleep, or just not paying attention. You were always concerned about our safety. You didn't just see us, Joe. You wanted to know us. Because of who you were, we grew to like you, and then we grew to love you. You became more than our neighbor. You were our friend. But let's not stop there.

At a time when many families are falling apart, you showed us true devotion. You loved your wife and daughter completely. We saw that, Joe, and we admired you for the man, the father, the husband you were. And let us not forget the pets. We'll never forget how tickled you got whenever the dogs made a fuss over you. "Come here," you would say to whomever was in hearing range. "Watch this." The dogs would be as quiet as little mice until you sounded the alarm on your red truck. Then their barking would rock the quiet neighborhood. "They can tell when it's me," you would say and laugh – a hearty laugh, a prideful laugh, a joyful laugh.

The dogs you loved so dearly will never hear you turn on and off that alarm again, Joe, and neither will we. We won't see you run out and get the mail or rush off to pick up your wife and daughter. We won't hear you laugh or ask us how we're doing. Those days are gone. Your voice is silent. A voice we will forever miss. The pain we feel is so great and will last so very long. And though we know that your suffering has ended and you have gone on to a better place, it is still very hard to say *Goodbye, Old Friend*.

A Note Of Thanks

From Henry B. Pender ("Uncle H.B.")

Dear Benny:

I could take this time to tell you the things that I remember about Uncle H. B. I could tell you how he allowed me to live with him and Aunt Bessie from the time I was fifteen years old until I graduated high school. I could tell you about the time I made him mad…really, really mad. It was just that once. But because Uncle H. B. was very slow to anger, when he did get mad…watch out! I could tell you about the last time I visited him in Jacksonville, Florida, where he lived with you and your wife, Karen. I could tell you of his laughter and his adoration for his wife of many years, Bessie Arrington Thompson-Pender. And not least, I could tell you about his longing and love for his family. But instead, today, I am going to put myself in his spirit and share with you what I think Uncle H. B. would say in this, his final hour. Being such an appreciative man, his first words would be:

"Thank you." Oh, he would throw back his head and fill an enormous space of air with his contagious laughter. "Lord," he would begin, "it sure is good to see y'all. I sure do appreciate you taking time outta your busy schedules just for little ole me. Now, I don't want you to worry 'bout me though, 'cause it's some kinda peaceful up here.

"Y'all know I have lived a long life, a good eighty-nine years. And my days of sickness were few. Each night I closed my eyes, I never feared not waking 'cause I knew the time was drawing nigh when I would join those who had gone on before me. I was ready to see my Bessie again. And the minute I got here, just like I imagined, she was fussing on account my journey took me such a while. But when I threw my arms 'round her, she hushed right up. Then, I looked up and Lord, who was coming but my youngest son, little Pender, grinning from ear-to-ear. I sure was glad to see him. When I turned 'round, there stood Albert, Jr., Joseph and Willie B. And if any of what I just now told you is hard to believe, I know you ain't go'n believe this. If I wasn't here I would have a hard time believing it myself. I felt a tap on my shoulder and before I could get both my feet in the same direction, there gazing right in my eyes were Tom, Eva, Christine, Jesse Lee, Jesse and Theresa looking as good as they ever did. I'm telling you, it was sure nice seeing 'em all again. Naw sir, it ain't go'n take me no time to feel right at home up here. So, you see, ain't no need for y'all to be sad 'bout me being gone and you sure don't have cause for worry.

"If y'all listen real hard you might be able to hear her. Can you hear her? Bessie's done started up her fussing again. She's calling after me. Listen."

"H.B.! Come on, here! Ain't we done waited on you plenty enough already? Lord, man! Come on. We're gitting ready to go!"

"I'm go'n run on now. But let me say this here before I go. Benny and Karen – thank you. You put up with me when I was healthy. We talked and laughed a lot. Benny, you and me even had words a little bit. When I got down with my illness and needed so much of your time, I was a little worried that I might be putting too much on you. Still, you made your home my home. You watched over and cared for me in a way I never would've imagined. I felt blessed to have you with me during my last days. I felt honored to call you my son. Uh oh. Do you hear her? Bessie's right steady calling after me. Listen."

"Come on, H. B.!"

"I gotta go. I thank you. I love you. I'm go'n miss you."

"Bye y'all."

Missed Opportunities

A Son, A Father, A Husband, A Friend

Dear Clara:

When I was told of James' death, I immediately thought of missed opportunities. The opportunity to sit by his bed and chat about old times. The opportunity to ask how he felt or what he was feeling. The opportunity to look into his eyes and see life...his life. The opportunity to witness a smile crack slowly across his lips, to hear his laughter, to offer a word of prayer or encouragement, to show compassion and concern, to know that he knew that I cared.

As a child, I was taught that we learn as much from death as we do from life. So, I asked myself what lessons are there to be learned from this death? What wisdom can be gained or shared? There are many, oh so many lessons that I've learned from having had this experience of missed opportunities. One I wish to share.

Take a moment to pause. Inside that pause think of at least three people that you have meant, intended, or planned to get around to visiting, to talking with but just haven't found the time. You think of them often, but things just keep getting in the way. Right? Don't put it off any longer. Today, make it your mission to tell somebody, anybody, one body how special they are to you. It need not be anything elaborate. Keep it simple – a humorous card, a short note, or a quick phone call to say hello. *Just do it.*

In life, James was someone's son, husband, father, uncle, cousin, and friend. He was important to many. He was loved. He will be missed. And, yes, in his passing, his death has taught me a big lesson – a lesson learned from *Missed Opportunities*.

To The Memory
Of Your Beloved Husband

Dear Bert:

My heart was truly saddened when my lovely sister, Grace, called to say that Willie B. had passed away. After our painfully brief conversation, my mind raced back many years to my first memories of Willie B. I remembered when, just a little girl, this tall, handsome man paid a visit to the farm. I remembered how he hugged my grandmother and how his laughter boomed with such force.

state of New Jersey and returned to your home in Greene County, North Carolina, where I witnessed how hard Willie B. worked to bounce back – how hard you worked to help him bounce back.

In spite of Willie B.'s many challenges, he weathered each storm with courage, determined to live a full and happy life. But when I think of this joy-filled man, I think of you, Bert. You brought him such an abundance of happiness. Your love for him was unquestionably present in every aspect of your being – in your eyes, in your laughter, in your humor, in your walk. How wonderful Willie B. must have felt knowing that he was loved so purely, so spiritually, so completely by you. And because of his love, trust and faith in you, I am certain that he believed you could face this difficult day – his final hour of rest. But most important, Bert, is what Willie B. wants for you at the end of the day – to move forward with your life with joy, vigor and love. Something tells me he is smiling down on you right now because he knows *you can do it.*

Years later, on a fall evening as we worked in the tobacco packhouse, Aunt Bessie, his mother, made a visit to the farm. But this time to deliver sad news. Willie B. was blind – blinded by a strange accident. Ma, Deddi and Aunt Bessie ended that visit claiming out loud that he was going to be fine. Faith is what Ma said they had to have. And it wasn't long before Willie B. recovered his eyesight. I remembered, as a young adult, receiving the phone call that he had had a stroke. And I remembered my visits with you and Willie B. after you retired, left the

Afterword

When You Think Of Me – Written As A Mother's Day Tribute To Mrs. Eva Brown-Arrington. Ma ("Mama Eva") – my mother, my grandmother, the joy of my life. She was a woman of many attributes – tender, strong, determined, spiritual, compassionate and fair. Ma taught as she believed – that one must be fair to *all* people. And she always put family first. No sacrifice was too great for her family. Her steel determination to persevere in the worst of times; her positive outlook on life; her belief in herself, in the goodness of people, and in God; and her love for *all* children inspired the writing of this poem.

A Moment Just For You – Written To Salute The Eightieth Birthday Of Mrs. Odessa Medley ("My Other Mother"). In 1992, when I was faced with my most difficult health challenge, Mrs. Medley ("Odessa") moved into my home and stayed by my side as close as a mother. She never ceased praying, never stopped hoping, believing, and doing *all* that she could to help bring about my recovery. I was honored to write this poem as a measure of my appreciation to such a magnificent human being who I will forever cherish.

My Friend – Written To Honor My Best Friend. As a child, growing up on a farm in rural Greene County, North Carolina, I often heard adults make the statement: "If you manage to get through this life with *one real good friend*…well, you have done something." More than thirty years ago, I met the person who would change that statement from an *old saying* to a *reality*. No, we were not instant soulmates. I doubt if I have had more heated arguments with another person. But as the years progressed, she taught me the meaning of the word *friend* by being a *friend*. She saw my flaws and tried to correct them. She discovered my weaknesses and tried to strengthen them. She uncovered my wounds and tried to heal them. She unveiled my fears and tried to chase them away. No matter the span of time that passes between our visits, whether lengthy or brief – a few weeks, a few days, a few hours, or just a few minutes on the phone catching up on the latest happenings, our time spent together always ends with me feeling that I have become a better person. So, if I was to end my journey right here, right now, my response to the elders of my youth is simply: "I – have – done – something. For Fredricka ("Fredi") Blackmon-Johnson – close as any sister, close as any blood kin – *is one real good friend*."

The Power Of Silence – Written To Salute Those (Women and Men) Who One Day Find The Courage To End The Cycle Of Violence Without Violence. This poem was inspired by a story told to me years ago. It is a story, I'm sure, that resonates with countless others who have used *The Power Of Silence* to end the cycle of violence in their lives. One day, a lady, after enduring years of abuse, without saying a word, without arguing or fighting, without making the same routine threats, waited for the opportune time when her mate was away, packed her bags and left…for good.

An Ending Of A Similar Kind – Inspired By The Story Of A-Nine-Year-Old. I wrote this poem after viewing a widely respected talk show host's airing of a visit to South Africa where Christmas gifts were given out to eagerly awaiting children. The story of a nine-year-old girl, whose mother was dying of AIDS, captured, held, and wouldn't let go of my heart. Though this child was thousands of miles away, through her story, I relived a part of my own life.

On the way to the hospital, the little girl was asked, "Do you think your mom is going to be all right?" The little girl started to respond, paused, seemed to rethink the question, then quietly said, "I don't know." I still replay in my thoughts and in my heart the painful dilemma of this little girl for it reminded me of the day my mother was taken by ambulance to the hospital. Before the ambulance pulled away, a friend asked me, "Do you think your ma is going to be all right?" Just like the nine-year-old South African girl, I started to respond, and paused, allowing my friend's question to echo in my ears. I was fifteen years old, and life, by then, had taught me, as I'm sure life had taught this nine-year-old girl, one very significant lesson…that there are no guarantees. Without shifting my eyes from the ambulance with its blinking red lights about to carry away my precious mother, I said quietly, barely above a whisper, "I don't know."

One Day – Inspired By The Teachings Of Mrs. Eva Brown-Arrington And Mrs. Ruth Jordan-Blackmon. This poem was read at the Wake of Mr. Melvin Hodges, at the funeral of my aunt, Mrs. Vivian Hill-Arrington, and was included in 'The Precious Memories Dedication To Ruth Jordan Blackmon.' *One Day* also appears in my first novel, *Stay The Course*, as a favorite gospel song of "Ma," one of the main characters.

Her Moment To Rest – Written In Honor Of Mrs. Lizzie Fleming Charles-Fuller. In the Acknowledgements of my first novel, *Stay The Course*, I write of Mother Fuller ("Miss Lizzie") … 'Alone, you educated eight children, persistently motivated the youth of my generation to believe in ourselves and to pursue our dreams; and, you are now paving the way for another generation by working to provide scholarships to deserving youth.' Though Mother Fuller was laid to rest on May 11, 2005, she left a generation well prepared to move forward.

On May 27, 2005, *Her Moment To Rest* was read at the Memorial Service for Mrs. Mildred Edwards, the mother of Mr. Wallace Edwards, a friend and alumnus of the Speight High School Graduating Class of 1971.

Before You Pull That Shade – Written To Celebrate The Life Of Mrs. Irene Speight. Mrs. Speight ("Miss Irene") was one of the mothers in the Stantonsburg, North Carolina, community where I grew up. She always had a smile for the children – *all children*…a smile that never faded. She was a joy to know, energetic, beautiful, stylish and authentic which inspired the writing of this poem.

I'm All Right – Written In Memory Of Mrs. Lee "Vesta" Mackey. Mrs. Mackey ("Miss Vesta") was another mother in the Stantonsburg, North Carolina, community that made the children feel right at home in *her home*. She was a funny, no-nonsense, comforting, free-spirited woman who always put out the welcome mat for me. Her strong will and warmth inspired the writing of this poem.

When The Morning Comes – Written In Memory Of Mrs. Ava ("Sutt") Barnes-Jennette. Ava was a childhood friend. We attended one of the same schools, Speight High, worked the farms together, played childhood games, sang in the church choir and walked the graveled streets of Stantonsburg on innumerable Saturdays and Sundays. We seldom saw each other after I moved to Alexandria, Virginia, in 1968. When I moved back to North Carolina in September of 2000, Ava and I only saw each other once at St. Luke Free Will Baptist Church in May of 2004. We never got a chance to talk privately. She came over and flashed me one of her beautiful grins. Someone diverted my attention away from her and when I looked again, Ava was gone. Weeks later, while visiting in Maryland, I received a call that Ava had been hospitalized. Days after returning to my home in Wilson, North Carolina, Ava passed away. Remembering her beautiful grin – a grin that was nearly identical to that of my younger sister, Ms. Theresa Louise Arrington, who passed away at a very young age – and her lovely spirit inspired this writing.

Joy In The Midst Of Sorrow – Written To Salute All Of Those Who Can Laugh Even When They Feel Like Crying. Although inspired by many, whenever I read this poem, my mind wanders back to the Chinn family who lost their oldest daughter, Ms. Mishann Dania Chinn, to violence. I was with them during the trial of one of the perpetrators. I was with them and witnessed the pain they endured at having to hear details of this horrific crime – details no parent should have to hear. But I also witnessed a level of strength in the Chinn family that seemed unimaginable. I witnessed their tenderness and sharing of kind words, their compassion and moments of laughter when I felt like crying. From the Chinn family – Mr. Michael Ronald, Mrs. Krishana ("Kris"), and Ms. Sheena Denae Chinn – I witnessed the true meaning of *Joy In The Midst Of Sorrow*.

A Tribute To The Life Of Ruby Swinson-Sanford – My dear friend, Mrs. Ruby Swinson-Sanford, loved my poetry and made a personal request that, on her final day, I read a poem just for her. I readily agreed totally unaware that the day to fulfill her final wish was so near. On March 5, 2005, on behalf of the 'First Grade Class of 1959,' the 'High School Graduating Class of 1971,' the Arrington, the Stephens, and the Yelverton families, I chose to read: *Joy In The Midst Of Sorrow*.

Whenever I Learn Another Mother Is Gone – A Letter Written To My Friend And Former Classmate, Pastor Mary Jo Edwards-Atkinson After The Passing Of Her Mother, Eldress Fannie Lee Edwards. Our lives go back so far I can't remember where it began. We attended the same church, attended some of the same schools, in particularly, North Greene Elementary School. We continue to see each other on occasion and our friendship has never waned. I guess some things just never end…they only keep getting better.

The Simple Things (In Memory Of A Special Wife) – A Letter Written To Mrs. Dietrich Ham-Diggs And Family During The Loss Of Their Sister, Mrs. Ethel Roberta ("Bert") Ham-Thompson. Bert was a comedian of sorts. She could make anyone laugh and often did even when she wanted to cry. This letter speaks of that person – the person I knew as a devoted wife, daughter, sister, friend, and one of my dearest cousins.

Remembering Your Mother, My Friend – A Letter Written To Mrs. Denise Blackmon-Thomas at the passing of her mother, my friend, Mrs. Ruth Elaine Jordan-Blackmon. Ruth and I were neighbors in the Stonehedge Community in Silver Spring, Maryland, for more than ten years. She is the only person who has read *every* manuscript I've written from start to finish several times – each time with the same heightened enthusiasm. Though I now wonder how and from where her enthusiasm came, especially when I look back over some of the original manuscripts…*they were bad*. But Ruth never wavered in her belief that my work was going to be published. She passed away seven months before my first novel, *Stay The Course*, was published. Still, she left me a special legacy to hold onto – her blessing.

The Things I Never Got To Say – Written As A Father's Day Tribute To Mr. Tom Arrington – my Deddi, my daddy, my grandfather, my provider. Deddi was a quiet man – a man of few words who was committed to his family and never wavered in that commitment. He rose every morning at dawn and worked the fields until the setting of the sun in hopes that his grandchildren could have a better life. He died before I was old enough to fully understand and appreciate the sacrifices he made. Writing this poem is my way of shouting to the world…"Thank you, Deddi!"

A Season For Pause – Written In Honor Of Mr. Ernest ("June", "Big E") Hall, Jr. June was the husband of my cousin, Mrs. Elizabeth Brown-Hall. I'll never forget the day he was given the unenviable responsibility of having to tell me that my most valued treasure, my grandmother, had passed away. The gentleness with which he delivered this painful news and the strength he showed have stayed with me. He never flinched, never gave way to his own emotions in the midst of my audible release of indescribable grief. He was a rock that I could hold onto during one of my worst moments. For that I will forever be thankful. His compassion, his self-confidence and his strength inspired the writing of this poem. His *Season For Pause* came on June 17, 2001.

A Moment Of Splendor – Written In Memory Of Mr. William ("Mr. Short") Ward At The Request Of His Wife, Mrs. Mary Lena ("Miss Mary Lena") Ward. Mr. Short and Miss Mary Lena were not just my acquaintances. They were longtime neighbors, friends and family. We lived within walking distance of each other in Greene County, North Carolina, where I was born, until I was in my early teens. The ages of their children nearly parallel those of my brothers, sisters, and me. We attended one of the same schools, North Greene Elementary, worked the farm together and often attended the same church, Bethel A.M.E. Zion Church. When Miss Mary Lena asked me to write a poem in memory of her husband, I did so with gratitude. We are and will forever remain as family.

One year after reading *A Moment Of Splendor* at Mr. Short's funeral, I shared this poem with my current neighbor, Mrs. Irene Riley, of Wilson, North Carolina, to honor the memory of her late husband, Mr. John Riley. What struck me while writing *A Moment Of Splendor* were the similarities of the two men – Mr. Riley and Mr. Ward. They both greeted me with the same smile in their voice, "Hey there, Lois. How're you doing?" They both were devoted family men. They both bore their illness with amazing dignity – one white, one black…the same kind spirit.

The Beauty In My Silence – Written In Memory, Honor And Tribute To The Life Of Pastor John Henry ("J. H.") Vines. Reverend Vines was my first Pastor. He became Pastor of St. Luke Free Will Baptist Church in 1958. I joined under his leadership at the age of thirteen. In 1968, I moved away from Stantonsburg, North Carolina, and saw little of Reverend Vines. After returning to North Carolina, I visited him once before he passed away in November of 2004. He will be remembered affectionately in the hearts of many.

The Beauty In My Silence was read on Saturday, October 29, 2005, to comfort Mrs. Inez Simms-Tyson at the Memorial Service for her baby son, Mr. Devon Simms.

I Don't Know – Written In Memory Of Mr. Ronnie Finch. Ronnie, a childhood friend, was the baby boy of his family. I spent little time with Ronnie, but quite a bit of time playing with his older sisters, Mrs. Betty Finch-Thomas and Mrs. Anne Finch-Artist. We attended one of the same schools, Speight High, the same church, St. Luke Free Will

Baptist Church, and knew most of the same people. I was deeply affected by the sudden loss of Ronnie. It caused me to relive the sorrow over the sudden loss of my brother, Mr. Jesse Ray Arrington, whose lively, fun-loving personality closely mirrored Ronnie's and inspired this writing.

I Don't Know was read at the Memorial Service for Mr. Devon Simms. Devon was the youngest child of my cousin, the late Mr. Elmo Simms and Mrs. Inez Simms-Tyson. He will be sorely missed by many, but especially by his mother; his daughter, Ms. Nikia Sharpe; his granddaughter, Ms. Kilira Sharpe; his sisters, Mrs. Bobbie Jean Simms-McKithan and Mrs. Bessie Mae Simms-Wooten; and his closest friends, horseback riding buddies and brothers, Mr. Ed Simms, Mr. Melvin ("Melt") Simms, Mr. Edgar Simms, and Mr. William Ward.

When You've Done Your Best – Written To Comfort The McGuthrie Family During The Loss Of Their Father, Husband, Son, Friend. I had just returned to my home ending my summer visit in Silver Spring, Maryland, with my best friend, Mrs. Fredricka Blackmon-Johnson, when she called to say Mr. Calvin McGuthrie had passed on. My thoughts went immediately to Mrs. Tasha Medley-Giles, his wife of many years, and Mrs. Shannon McGuthrie-Fields, his daughter who had been the primary caregiver, spending long hours nursing her father. This poem was inspired by Shannon's dedication and selfless giving of herself.

A Note Of Thanks – A Letter Written To Mr. Benjamin ("Benny") Thomas. In August, 1968, after the death of my grandmother, Mrs. Eva Brown-Arrington, Uncle H. B. ("Henry B. Pender") gave his nod of approval for me to live with him and his wife, my Aunt Bessie. I never felt that I did enough to show my gratitude to Uncle H. B. for opening up his home to me – not in a way that I would be able to do today. When he became ill, Benny was the major caregiver. I learned tons from watching Benny. He showed such patience, courage and compassion during Uncle H. B.'s illness. Benny's dedication to his mother, Aunt Bessie, and his stepfather, Uncle H. B., is the energy behind the writing of *A Note Of Thanks*.

Missed Opportunities – A Letter Written To Mrs. Clara ("Snook") Joyner. I missed the opportunity to spend time with my cousins during the loss of James ("Snook") Joyner, husband, father, son and friend. I occasionally still see his wife, Clara, and I hope that there will be few, or no more, missed opportunities.

To The Memory Of Your Beloved Husband – A Letter Written To Mrs. Ethel Roberta ("Bert") Ham-Thompson. Bert truly loved and was devoted to her husband, Mr. Willie B. Thompson. She demonstrated remarkable strength during his illness, in his passing and the years that followed before her passing. In our last conversation, Bert mentioned this letter. She said, from time-to-time, she would read it just to lift her spirit.

Goodbye Old Friend – A Letter Written To Mr. Joseph ("Joe") Johns. Joe and his family were my neighbors for nearly ten years in the Stonehedge Community in Silver Spring, Maryland. Joe was a lively, happy man – one of the most color-blind people I knew. If you were a decent, upstanding human being…that was enough for Joe. The rest – color, ethnicity, sex and religion didn't matter. Joe, indeed, led by example. He set a benchmark for others to live by. This letter to his family portrays the Joe I knew, liked and admired.

In Memory

This section of *Words Of Comfort* is set aside not for the most popular, or the richest, or the most beautiful, or the most successful. It is a special part of the book intended to send a message to the loved ones of the dearly departed...one very important message: That you were here, that you were loved, that your life mattered.

Loving Family

Clara ("Grandma Clara") Barnes

Charlie and Candice Arrington-Dickinson

Jacob ("Jake") and Mary Jane Brown

Tom and Eva ("Feet") Brown-Arrington

Ruby Christine Arrington-Swinson

Jesse R. Arrington

Theresa Louise Arrington and Baby Boy Arrington

Ola Mae Barnes-Arrington

Jesse Lee and Vivian Hill-Arrington

Sherry Arrington Brown-Schnell

Lena Atlas

James Brooks

Allen and Clyde Stanley-Brown

Jacob, Jr. ("Buddy") and Emma Brown

Mattie Gray Brown-Blake

Frank ("Bud") Brown

Minnie Lee Brown-Farmer

Roosevelt Brown

Columbus ("Balim") Brown

Joe ("Shorty") Brown

Ginny Brown

Ruben and Louvenia ("Pat") Brown-Simms

Raleigh and Nora Simms-Stackhouse

Elmo Simms

Devon Simms

Arthur ("Joe") Simms

Raymond Simms

LaToya Denise Simms

Tomeka Denise Simms

Henry ("H. B.") and Bessie Arrington-Thompson-Pender

Albert Thompson, Jr.

Joseph Thomas (Thompson)

Willie B. and Ethel Roberta Ham-Thompson

Mary ("Grandma Mary") Crumel-Ellis

Golden and Colina ("Tince") Harper-Joyner

James Alexander ("Snook") Joyner

James Alexander Joyner, Jr.

Richard Lee Joyner

Willie Hodges and Bessie Mae Pender Hodges-Speight

Lucretia Ann Pender-Hodges

Orlando ("Pete") Pender

Ernest ("Mr. Brownie") Hall, Sr. and Ometer Rodgers-Hall

Ernest ("June", "Big E") Hall, Jr.

Clarence ("Bud") Hodges

Annie Mae Hodges

Glossie Mae Hodges-Fields

Melvin ("Melt") Hodges

Jean Stephens-Becker

Elijah and Carnie Baker

Betty Baker-Body

Clarence Baker

Preston and Sarah ("Miss Doll") Baker-Yelverton

Esther Yelverton-Artis

Freddie Yelverton

Gerline ("Girlie") Brown-McBroom

Louis and Pearlie Ann Ham-Locus-Barnes

James Harvestus Locus

Russell Locus

Ernest and Ida Ham

Hettie Bell Ham

James and Mary Frances Ham

Bessie Mae Ham-Elder

Lenzie and Hettie Bell Ham

William Pete and Appie Pauline Artis-Ham

Claude Lee Ham

Delmarie Ham

Elouise Ham

Lonnie Ham

William Pete Ham, Jr.

Melvadine Ham-Ward

John and Rebecca Swinson

Bessie Swinson-Artis

Johnnie ("Puncho") Swinson

Ruby Swinson-Sanford

Bernice and Frances Swinson-Winstead

Anne Swinson-Winstead

"Tootsie" Swinson-Winstead

Florence and James Earl Hackley

Bobby Hackley

Martha ("Mue") Harris-Greene

Silas Lester ("Bue") Harris

Nebraska Harris-Dickerson

Rosetta Harris-Williams

Bonnie Ellison

Dorothy Ellison

Modree Ellison-Turner

Robert and Mamie Ellison

Qubia and Minnie Jones

Henry and Eloise Jones

Richard and Ritter Vellamy-Jones

Samuel ("Sam") Jones

Lillie Bynum-Barnes

Irene Bynum-Bedford

Lillie Mae Bynum-Dixon

Martha Purdie

Avie Davis Jones-Tucker

James Woodrow and Alberta ("Mu") Kee-Crockett

Arthur Kemp

Clarence Kemp

Cynthia Kemp

Robert Malloy

Lawrence Williams

Dear Neighbors and Friends

Matthew Alston

Melford ("Odell") and Helen Artis

Beulah Mae Artis

Diane Artis

Douglas Melvin Artis

Lois Jean Artis

Nathaniel ("Mr. Boog") Artis

Pauline ("Miss Pauline") Artis

Nathan and Fannie Spruill-Artis

George, Sr. and Virginia Artis-Bunch

Alexander and Cora Artis

Helen Rophteen Artis-Johnson

Willie Mae Atkinson

Kenneth ("Kenny") Baggage

T. J. ("Pastor") Baltimore

Hattie Barnes

Ruth Barnes

James and Ava ("Sutt") Barnes-Jennette

Ernest and Elizabeth Barnes

Johnny Earl ("Earl") Barnes

Thomas ("Elder Thomas") and Minnie ("Miss Minnie") Barnes

Ben J. Barnes

Jennie Barnes-Williams

Moses Barron

Lenwood Junior ("Sunny Boy") Barron

Milton Earl Beamon

Paul Beamon

Gaye B. Becker

Margaret Bishop

Tamika Black

Claude and Sally Walker-Jordan

Ruth Elaine Jordan-Blackmon

Joe Bland

Maggie Bozeman

Genevie Bowling-Williams

Sandra Williams-Lewis

Barbara Braye

Robert Bridgers

J. C. Brown

Walter and Marion Browning, Sr.

Sherman and Zenobia Browning-Grundy

Alphonso (Dr.) and Fredricka Hansborough-Burwell, Sr.

Gregory Burwell

Egbert and Alcyone Campbell-Facey

Zenobia Campbell-Lewis

Michael Cherry

Mishann Dania Chinn

Andrew T. Jackson

Albert Lassiter

Jacqueline Matthews

Thomas Jefferson Matthews

Betram Nicholls

Alice Williams

Rommie Coley

Alex and Jessie Bell Council

Charles ("Mr. Charlie") Council

Thelma Lois Council

Alice Cummings

Howard Daniels

Levi and Amanda Ward-Daniels

James Earl Daniels

Jack and Pinky Davis

Felix Duran

David and Calisie ("Miss Calisie") Jones-Diggs

Never Duncan, Jr.

Madeline Duggan

James Earl Edwards

John ("Pie") and Fannie Lee ("Eldress") Barnes-Edwards

Anthony Edwards

Rosa ("Mother Rosa") Edwards

Mildred Edwards

Harry ("Pa Ellis") and Luetta Ellis

Oscar Ellis

Billie Ray Ellis

John H. Ellis

John Lee Ellis

Samuel B. Ethridge

Eileen Ewing

Obediah Farmer

Reginald ("Reggie") Edwards

Charlie Farmer

Eddie and Rosa Finch

Eloise Finch

Ronnie L. Finch

Annie Louise Finch-Edwards

Joshua and Lizzie Jones-Fleming

Douglas ("Bro. Doug") Fleming

Lizzie ("Mother Fuller") Fleming-Charles-Fuller

Aleseya Re'Shele ("Le Le") Barnes-Daniel

Demall R. Irby

Stella Ann Fleming

Willie F. Freeman

Michael Ford

Morris and Frances Gavin

Edith Goldman

Chalmer ("Mr. Buck") and Judy ("Miss Judy Gray") Grantham

Mabel Melvin-Green

Thomas and Ida Hall

Thomas ("Bud") Hall, Jr.

Lee and Belle Harper

JoAnne Harper

"Woody" Harrington

Melvin and Esther Lee Dixon-Harris

James Titus Harris

Elmore and Hyacinth ("Hiccie") Harris-Medley

Dorman Medley, Sr.

Destiny Pinto

Pearl Gatling

Tassie Harris-Andrews

Sandra Harris

Herbert Horne

William Douglas Horne, Sr.

Roosevelt ("Mr. Buster") and Suzanne Howard

Willie King

Phillip Earl Ingram

James and Carrie ("Miss Carrie") Isler

Tyronne Isler

Tanji Jackson

Joseph ("Joe") A. Johns

George W. Jones

Leroy Leveston

Leon Little

Leroy Lovitte

Morris Nelson ("Mar Nelson") Lovitte

Lee "Vesta" Mackey

Doris ("Tootie") Mackey

Letha Bell Mercer

William Marshall and Catherine McGuthrie

Calvin Maurice McGuthrie

Rodwell, Sr. and Theotis McGregor-McNeill

Pearl McNeill-Townsend

Francis and Phyllis Mesteth

J.T. Mitchell

James ("Hoop") Earl Mitchell

Carmen ("Candy") Olivia Newsom

Valena Newsome-Miller

James Walter and Geneva Barnes-Newsome

Cleveland Arlester ("Mr. Clee") and Alice Mae Guess-Newsome

Pessie L. Pender

Alma Gray Pender-Shirley

Marvin Pender

Frank, Jr. and Corrine Pope

Javetta Richardson-Piper

Cynthia Ann Wilson-Putnam

Wellford and Viola Reid

Charles Arthur Reid

Peter Ridenour

John Riley

Mamie Robertson

Missouri Robinson

David Lee Sanders

Ricky Earl Sanders

Rita Shakespeare

Gail Charmayne Sharpe

Bethezel ("Bettie") Chappelle-Shipman

Freeman and Irene Jones-Speight

Ethel Irene Speight

Freeman Speight, Jr.

Minnie Gray Speight

Eva Earlene Speight

George ("Billy") Speight, Jr.

Raymond ("Ray") Speight

Lucille ("Sis") Speight

Sadie Speight

T. J. ("T") Speight

Alice Speight

Bertha Speight

Geneva Sutton-Speight

Walter ("Leeboy") Speight, Sr.

Linwood Spells

Burl Street

Florence Tancil

Horace and Anna Tancil

Christine ("Chris") Louise Taylor

Veronica Taylor

Jim Thigpen

Lessie Thomas

Herbert Tyson

Hubert and Belle Tyson

Levi Tyson

Raul Viegas

J. P. Moran and Annie Mae Best-Vines

John Henry ("Reverend J. H.") and Adelle Bullock-Vines

Dave ("Mr. Dave") Ward

Elijah ("Mr. Bunk") and Geneva Hamilton-Ward

William J. (" Mr. Short") Ward

William ("Spookie") Ward

Roscoe, Sr. and Ruby Ward

Roscoe Lee Ward, Jr.

Sally Ward

Sarah Ward

Virginia ("Ms. Meat: Eldress") Ward

Theodore ("Teddy") Ward

Marty Ware

Marie O. Warren

James P. Watkins, Sr.

James P. Watkins, Jr.

Richard T. Watkins

Allan M. West

Sam and Minnie West

John White

Ola Mae Ellis-White

Cecil Jerrill and Willomena Hines-White

Curtis ("Kurt") Lee Williams

Lacy Williams

Manna ("Miss Manna") Williams

Herbert ("Mr. Babe") Williams

Robert Williams

Mercedes Williams

Tonya Williams

Martha Winstead-Walker

Walter and Emma Ford-Winstead

Nancy B. Winstead

Walter Lee Winstead

Willie Lee Winstead

Jake and Lennie Perry-Wise

Thomas Jake and Annie Wise

Ruth Wolff

Barbara Wood

John Lee ("Mr. John Lee") Woodard

Johnny and Nina ("Miss Nina") Harris-Woodard

Anthony Dru Wright

FEB 1 2010

LaVergne, TN USA
27 August 2009
156195LV00002B